For the Teacher

This reproducible study guide to use in conjunction with *Stargirl* consists of lessons for guided reading. Written in chapter-by-chapter format, the guide contains a synopsis, pre-reading activities, vocabulary and comprehension exercises, as well as extension activities to be used as follow-up to the novel.

In a homogeneous classroom, whole class instruction with one title is appropriate. In a heterogeneous classroom, reading groups should be formed: each group works on a different novel at its reading level. Depending upon the length of time devoted to reading in the classroom, each novel, with its guide and accompanying lessons, may be completed in three to six weeks.

Begin using NOVEL-TIES for guided reading by distributing the novel and a folder to each child. Distribute duplicated pages of the study guide for students to place in their folders. After examining the cover and glancing through the book, students can participate in several pre-reading activities. Vocabulary questions should be considered prior to reading a chapter or group of chapters; all other work should be done after the chapter has been read. Comprehension questions can be answered orally or in writing. The classroom teacher should determine the amount of work to be assigned, always keeping in mind that readers must be nurtured and that the ultimate goal is encouraging students' love of reading.

The benefits of using NOVEL-TIES are numerous. Students read good literature in the original, rather than in abridged or edited form. The good reading habits will be transferred to the books students read independently. Passive readers become active, avid readers.

Novel-Ties® are printed on recycled paper.

SYNOPSIS

As Leo Borlock explains, the Mica Area High School students are blasé about everything. They live in a newly created city, built around an electronics company, where conformity is expected of adults and young people. Suddenly, a newcomer shatters the status quo. On the first day of school, a girl walks into the cafeteria and starts strumming a ukulele. She is dressed in unusual clothes, sings "Happy Birthday" to a shy boy, and strolls through the room completely at ease. Suddenly, the room is buzzing with amazed speculation. Who is this tenth grader with such self-assurance? Stargirl's fellow students at Mica are both fascinated and repelled by her individuality.

The new girl calls herself Stargirl Caraway. Prior to coming to Mica, she had been home-schooled, which might account for her unique personality. But as Leo finds out, Stargirl's exuberance, talent for friendship, and seeming indifference to the opinions of others mark her as a special person. When the captain of the cheerleaders taps her for the squad, nearly everyone wants to be Stargirl's friend. And Leo, though he will not quite admit it to himself or to his best pal Kevin, wants to be something more to her.

Stargirl gives gifts to complete strangers, cries for the troubles of others, and never forgets the miracle of just being alive. She teaches Leo to listen to the silent music that surrounds them. Her joy, however, makes her oblivious to the trouble that is brewing. Her eccentricities offend some people, particularly Hillari Kimble, one of Mica's most popular students. When Stargirl's generosity of spirit leads her to cheer for the rival team, her schoolmates declare her a traitor and begin a shunning campaign against her. On the same day that someone throws a tomato at her, Leo receives a love note from Stargirl. Their budding romance throws Leo into conflict with himself: is a liasion with Stargirl worth the censure of his peers?

In an effort to resolve his inner conflict, Leo consults with Archie Brubaker, a paleontologist who has been his friend and mentor. He advises Leo to appreciate Stargirl as a rare, unique individual, or reject her and cling to the herd. Although he wants Stargirl's affection, Leo is not ready to be rejected by his friends and fellow students.

In an attempt to solve his own personal crisis, Leo convinces Stargirl to change so that she will fit in with the crowd. Even after Stargirl attempts to comply, the other

students continue to shun her. At last, Stargirl plays her trump card. She triumphs at the statewide oratorical championship, mesmerizing the audience with her fluency and profundity. Expecting to be adored on her return to Mica, Stargirl is devastated when almost nobody, but her best friend Dori, is there to greet her.

Stargirl at last gives up on popularity. Knowing that he is embarrassed by her, she also gives up on Leo. Soon she will be only a memory in the city of Mica. Yet, before she and her family move on to another state, she has one final, unforgettable night as the unofficial queen of the Ocotillo Ball, leading the students in a dance out of the school building into the star-filled night.

Some years later, Leo still mulls over the mystery of Stargirl Caraway. He realizes that she gave him the precious gift of appreciating the small things of everyday life. The story ends as Leo hopes for a second chance to encounter this magical human being.

About the Author

Jerry Spinelli was born in Norristown, Pennsylvania in 1941. He began writing when he was sixteen, publishing his first poem in a local newspaper. He graduated from Gettysburg College in 1963 and received a Master's Degree in 1964 from Johns Hopkins University. He was in the Naval Reserve from 1966 to 1972. In 1977 Spinelli married a children's book author. The couple have seven children.

Spinelli began by writing books for adults. He later found that he was more successful when he wrote about the pleasure and pain of growing up. The author says that his childhood memories, along with the experiences of his own children, are the inspiration for his writing. He believes that every child is a Huckleberry Finn, exploring the river of life. In each of his books, Spinelli tries to capture a sense of wonder and discovery.

In 1991 he won the Newbery Award for *Maniac Magee*, and in 1998, *Wringer* was named a Newbery Honor book.

PRE-READING ACTIVITIES

1. Preview the book by reading the title and the author's name and by looking at the illustration on the cover. What do you think the book will be about? Have you read any other books by the same author?

2. Stargirl, the central character in this novel, is a teenager who has a unique personality. How would a person who does not conform be treated in your school or among your friends? Do you think people should be expected to conform or should they be encouraged to express their own unique qualities?

3. Read the brief biography of the author Jerry Spinelli on page two of this study guide and do some additional research to learn more about his life. As you read the novel and the interview that follows it, determine how Spinelli's life experiences and beliefs may have influenced the story.

4. Do you or anyone you know hide your true individuality in order to fit into the crowd? Do you think other people can see through this mask? What benefits and disadvantages can result from this behavior?

5. The narrator of this book faces a crisis of values and loyalty. He must choose between the good opinion of a large group and the love of one special person. What do you think a person might do when faced with this type of dilemma? What criteria might help the person make the best choice?

6. Do you think we should choose friends who are similar to us, or different? What might we learn from each kind of relationship?

7. *Stargirl* explores the issue of peer pressure. What are some examples of the ways that peers influence your behavior? Have you ever observed other people behaving in a manner that is contrary to their own values because of peer pressure? Is peer pressure ever beneficial to individuals?

PORCUPINE NECKTIE; CHAPTERS 1 – 5

Vocabulary: Draw a line from each word on the left to its definition on the right. Then use the numbered words to answer the questions below.

1.	dramatic	a.	strange
2.	noteworthy	b.	continuing forever
3.	weird	c.	of poor quality; cheap; shoddy
4.	sleazy	d.	final; perfect
5.	vague	e.	deserving special attention
6.	elusive	f.	exciting; striking
7.	perpetual	g.	difficult to explain or grasp
8.	ultimate	h.	not precisely felt or known

. . . .

1. Which word might describe an animal that hunters find hard to track?

   ____

2. Which word might be used in a description of a haunted house?

   ____

3. Which word might describe a wheel that never stops turning?

   ____

4. Which word might describe something that is carelessly and inexpensively made?

   ____

5. Which word might be used in a newspaper article that discusses the building of a national monument?

   ____

6. Which word might be used by a patient to describe an illness with no identifiable symptoms?

   ____

7. Which word might describe the final verdict of a jury after a long trial?

   ____

8. Which word might describe the thrilling rescue of a person from a sinking ship?

   ____

Porcupine Necktie; Chapters 1 – 5 (cont.)

> Read to find out what the students at Mica Area High think of Stargirl.

Questions:

1. How did the gift of the porcupine tie prepare the way for other events?
2. Why did Stargirl immediately become the target of gossip at school?
3. Why were Leo and Kevin especially excited by the presence of this new student?
4. According to Hillari Kimble, why was Stargirl at Mica Area High?
5. In what way did the moonlight suggest to Leo "a sense of the otherness of things"? Why was night the time when Leo thought most about Stargirl?
6. In what ways was Wayne Parr typical of the entire Mica student body?
7. Why did many spectators suddenly come to a Mica football game?

Questions for Discussion:

1. Why do you suppose that Leo refused to sign up Stargirl for an interview on "Hot Seat"?
2. Why do you think Stargirl sang to individual students on their birthdays?
3. What do you think Leo learned when he followed Stargirl around the town?
4. Why do you think the students at Mica kept developing theories about Stargirl, but made no attempt to get to know her?
5. In your opinion was Stargirl a loner or did she want to befriend her new classmates?
6. Do you know anyone like Stargirl? Would you like to know someone like her?

Literary Devices:

I. *Simile*—A simile is a figure of speech which compares two unlike objects using the words "like" or "as." For example:

> We did not know what to make of her [Stargirl]. In our minds we tried to pin her to a corkboard like a butterfly, but the pin merely went through and away she flew.

What is being compared?

____

What does this reveal about the students at Mica? What does this reveal about Stargirl?

____

____

____

Porcupine Necktie; Chapters 1 – 5 (cont.)

II. *Metaphor*—A metaphor is an implied or suggested comparison between two unlike objects. For example:

> She [Stargirl] seemed marooned in a sea of staring, buzzing faces.

What is being compared?

____

What does this reveal about the way the students at Mica reacted to Stargirl?

____

____

III. *Point of View*—Point of view in literature refers to the voice telling the story. It could be one of the characters or the author narrating. From whose point of view is this story told?

____

Why do you think the story was not told from Stargirl's point of view?

____

____

IV. *Cliffhanger*—A cliffhanger in literature refers to a device used in silent, serialized films in which an episode ended at a moment of suspense. In a book it is often found at the end of a chapter. What is the cliffhanger at the end of Chapter Five?

____

Science Connection:

Do some research to learn about desert plants. Find illustrations and written descriptions of the prickly pear and saguaro cacti. Why are these plants suited to the desert environment?

Writing Activity:

Think of five questions you would ask Stargirl during an interview. How might she have answered these questions? Write a script containing your questions and her possible responses.

CHAPTERS 6 – 10

Vocabulary: Synonyms are words with similar meanings. Draw a line from each word in column A to its synonym in column B. Then use the words in column A to fill in the blanks in the sentences below.

A	B
1. amorphous	a. dead
2. bafflement	b. freedom
3. blithely	c. joyful
4. deceased	d. nearness
5. dormant	e. shapeless
6. elated	f. cheerfully
7. liberation	g. perplexity
8. proximity	h. sleeping

. . . .

1. Certain animals, such as bears, remain _________________ during the cold months of winter.

2. Because of the _________________ of my house to the school, I often go home for lunch.

3. The Civil War hastened the _________________ of African-American slaves.

4. Our team was _________________ when we won the last game of the season.

5. The snowman melted in the thaw, becoming a(n) _________________ blob of snow.

6. The newspapers carried many obituaries about the _________________ man.

7. The children skipped _________________ down the street, glad that vacation had at last begun.

8. Even the clever detective admitted her _________________ at the odd assortment of clues in the case.

> Read to find out about the impact Stargirl has made on Mica Area High.

Chapters 6 – 10 (cont.)

Questions:

1. Why did Leo and Kevin pay a visit to Archie?
2. What did Stargirl's solution to the problem of Hillari's birthday reveal about her?
3. What was Archie's relationship to Stargirl?
4. Why didn't Hillari drop Stargirl's pet rat down the stairwell?
5. How was it revealed that Stargirl had gained great popularity at Mica High?
6. How did Stargirl change life at Mica High?
7. Why were several of Stargirl's acts of generosity considered inappropriate by some of the townspeople? How did two of these sympathetic gestures create tension?

Questions for Discussion:

1. Do you think people should select a name for themselves, as Stargirl has done?
2. How do you think home-schooling could affect the way a child learns? What might be the benefits and drawbacks of learning at home?
3. What do you suppose Archie meant when he said of Stargirl, "She is us more than we are us. She is, I think, who we really are"?
4. Why do you suppose Archie did not give specific advice to the boys? Why did he often speak in riddles?
5. Why do you imagine Archie wanted Leo and Kevin to observe Stargirl? What did he hope they would learn?
6. Why do you think people reacted so strongly to Stargirl either in a positive or negative way? Why was it hard to be indifferent to her?
7. In what ways do you act as an individual, and in what ways do you follow the crowd?

Literary Devices:

I. *Analogy*—An analogy is a comparison of two or more similar objects which suggests that if they are alike in certain respects, they will probably be alike in other ways as well. For example:

> They lie dormant and waiting, these mud frogs, for without water their lives are incomplete, they are not fully themselves. For many months they sleep like this within the earth. And then the rain comes. And a hundred pairs of eyes pop out of the mud, and at night a hundred voices call across the moonlit water….It was wonderful to see, wonderful to be in the middle of: we mud frogs awakening all around.

How were the students at Mica High analogous to mud frogs?

Chapters 6 – 10 (cont.)

II. *Foreshadowing*—Foreshadowing refers to the hints or clues that an author provides to suggest later events in the story. What do you think Leo foreshadowed when he said, "It was a golden age, those few weeks in December and January. How could I know that when the end came, I would be in the middle of it?"

____

____

III. *Personification*—Personification is a literary device in which an author grants human qualities to a nonhuman object. For example:

> Señor Saguaro was a cactus, a thirty-foot-tall giant that towered over the toolshed in the backyard. It had two arms high on the trunk. One stuck straight out; the other made a right turn upward, as if waving "adiós!" The waving arm was green from the elbow up; all else was brown, dead. Much of the thick, leathery skin along the trunk had come loose and crumpled in a heap about the massive foot: Señor Saguaro had lost his pants. Only his ribs, thumb-thick vertical timbers, held him up.

What is being personified?

____

What does this suggest about the significance of this cactus plant?

____

____

IV. *Simile*—What is being compared in the following simile?

> From the moment we arrived at school the next day, the atmosphere bristled like cactus paddles.

____

What does this suggest about the mood at school?

____

____

Writing Activities:

1. Write about a time when your actions, like those of Stargirl, were misunderstood. Describe the situation and its outcome.

2. Write about a person in your life who has been a teacher in the deepest sense of that word. What have you learned from this individual? What other contributions has this person made to your life?

CHAPTERS 11 – 15

Vocabulary: Use the context to determine the meaning of the underlined word in each of the following sentences. Then draw a line from each word to its definition below.

- Because she was <u>oblivious</u> to the coming storm, the hiker continued climbing up the mountainside.

- The doctor prescribed a liquid medication to <u>suppress</u> the child's coughing.

- The jury had difficulty reaching a <u>verdict</u> but finally decided that the accused man was innocent.

- When my sister has to give an oral report, she always becomes <u>flustered</u> and does not perform well.

- The <u>hostility</u> of the crowd caused the politician to leave the podium after several minutes.

- When the war ended, you could see scenes of <u>jubilation</u> on every street corner.

- The germs brought by the settlers <u>annihilated</u> the native population of the region.

- The <u>convoy</u> of tanks rolled through the desert, stretching as far as the eye could see.

. . . .

1. oblivious		a. decision
2. suppress		b. completely destroyed
3. verdict		c. group acting as a protective escort
4. flustered		d. antagonism or anger
5. hostility		e. hold or keep down
6. jubilation		f. not aware or conscious
7. annihilated		g. embarrassed
8. convoy		h. elation; triumphant joy

Chapters 11 – 15 (cont.)

> Read to find out what happens when Stargirl takes the "hot seat."

Questions:

1. How did the recent fanaticism about winning games show that the MAHS students had misunderstood Stargirl's message?

2. How was Stargirl's reaction to the MAHS vs. Red Rock game consistent with her responses to other situations?

3. Why did Leo have a bad feeling before Stargirl was interviewed for "Hot Seat"?

4. What did Leo mean when he said that Stargirl was taking the "Hot Seat" literally? Why did she behave in this manner?

5. Why were Kevin and Leo sorry they put Stargirl on "Hot Seat"?

6. Why did the MAHS students turn on Stargirl during their losing game with Glendale?

7. Why did Leo run from the lunchroom? Did his actions reveal his true feelings about Stargirl?

Questions for Discussion:

1. What does it mean for a person to "have no ego"? Do you think this is a positive or a negative character trait?

2. Why do you suppose Stargirl never suspected she had been the victim of a trick by the MAHS cheerleaders?

3. Why do you imagine people allow themselves to be humiliated on shows such as "Hot Seat"? What does this eagerness to participate in such programs reveal about people?

4. What point do you think Archie was trying to make about the prehistoric skull that belonged to one of our early ancestors?

Chapters 11 – 15 (cont.)

Literary Device: Metaphor

What is being compared in the following metaphor?

> But on this day [the day of the *Hot Seat* show] the thrill was missing.
> I felt only a dark dread snaking along the cables.

Why is this an apt comparison?

Cooperative Learning Activity:

Work with a small group of your classmates to discuss the questions that follow. Record your group's responses. Compare your responses with those of other groups in your classroom.

- Are the values of any particular person likely to be different from the values held by a group of people?
- What kinds of problems can occur when an individual has a different value system from his or her peer group?
- Can Stargirl maintain her own values and still be accepted by the students of Mica Area High School?

Writing Activity:

Imagine that you are Stargirl and write a journal entry describing your emotions on the day of the game between MAHS and Glendale.

CHAPTERS 16 – 20

Vocabulary: Antonyms are words with opposite meanings. Draw a line from each word in column A to its antonym in column B. Then use the words in column A to complete the sentences below.

<u>A</u>   <u>B</u>

1. acquainted   a. fertile

2. barren   b. free

3. detached   c. unfamiliar

4. dilapidated   d. harmonious

5. immobilize   e. loyalty

6. raucous   f. preserved

7. treason   g. joined

. . . .

1. We bought an old, __________________ house because it was inexpensive and we could do the repairs ourselves.

2. The veterinarian had to __________________ the dog before she could do a complete examination.

3. The __________________ screech of the crow outside my window woke me from a sound sleep.

4. We had scarcely become __________________ with our new neighbor before she sold her house and left town.

5. The __________________ land was useless for farming or grazing.

6. Weeks after Halloween had passed, my little brother finally __________________ the stickers of witches and jack o' lanterns from our windows.

7. The spy was sentenced and imprisoned for the crime of __________________ against the nation.

Chapters 16 – 20 (cont.)

> Read to find out why Leo has a hard time being Stargirl's boyfriend.

Questions:

1. What did Leo mean when he said of Stargirl, "I was more comfortable with her as history than as person"?

2. Why did Stargirl take Leo to the enchanted place? Why did Leo have feelings both of success and failure after his visit to this place?

3. Why was Leo initially unaware that he and Stargirl were receiving the silent treatment? How did he feel when he realized what was happening?

4. What choice did Archie want Leo to make? How did he try to help him make this important decision?

5. How did Stargirl and Leo disagree about the significance of good deeds?

6. Why did Leo conclude that Stargirl gave him the porcupine necktie?

Questions for Discussion:

1. Why do you suppose Stargirl wanted Leo to handle Cinnamon?

2. Do you accept Kevin's explanation for the reason students were shunning Stargirl? Might there be other reasons for their treatment of her?

3. Have you ever experienced a moment when you felt at one with the universe? Do you think this is a desirable state to achieve?

4. Do you think Leo should reject Stargirl or continue to ignore his classmates? What would you do?

Literary Device: Symbolism

A symbol in literature refers to an object, person, or place that represents an idea or set of ideas. With your classmates, discuss the symbolic meanings of the moon and Sẽnor Saguaro. Does anything else in the novel function as a symbol?

Chapters 16 – 20 (cont.)

Literary Elements:

I. *Setting*—Setting refers to the time and place in which the events of a story take place. Reread the passage about the desert in Chapter Seventeen. How did the description of the desert setting give greater meaning to the conversation between Leo and Stargirl?

II. *Conflict*—Conflict refers to the clash of opposing people, objects, or ideas. In literature, a character may face any of the following kinds of conflicts:

- person *vs.* person

- person *vs.* nature

- person *vs.* self

What kinds of conflicts have you encountered so far in this novel?

____

____

____

____

____

Science Connections:

1. Do some research to learn about the Sonoran Desert in Arizona. Find out about its climate and landscape and about the animals and plants that live there. How is it different from the Sahara Desert? Find pictures of the following desert plants mentioned in the book: saguaro cactus; yucca; beavertail; prickly pear and barrel cacti; buckhorn, staghorn, and devil's fingers; ocotillo; and Maricopas.

2. Humankind's evolution has been divided into specific eras, or phases. Do some research on human evolution to learn about people at each period of prehistory. Choose one of these eras and find out as much detailed information as possible. Then present your findings to your classmates in the form of an oral report.

Writing Activity:

Write about a time when an important friendship was tested by other people or events. What factors threatened the friendship? What was the ultimate outcome?

CHAPTERS 21 – 27

Vocabulary: Analogies are equations in which the first pair of words has the same relationship as the second pair of words. For example: SLIM is to THIN as MOURNFUL is to SAD. Both pairs of words are synonyms. Choose the best word from the Word Box to complete each of the analogies below.

<table>
<tr><td colspan="3">WORD BOX</td></tr>
<tr><td>conferred</td><td>extravagance</td><td>tentatively</td></tr>
<tr><td>confirm</td><td>facetiously</td><td>zeal</td></tr>
<tr><td>distinct</td><td>jostle</td><td></td></tr>
</table>

1. ARGUED is to QUARRELED as _________________ is to CONSULTED.

2. _________________ is to FORCEFULLY as STINGILY is to GENEROUSLY.

3. HERO is to COURAGE as SPENDTHRIFT is to _________________.

4. AWKWARDLY is to GRACEFULLY as _________________ is to SERIOUSLY.

5. VAGUE is to CONFUSION as _________________ is to CLARITY.

6. CHEERLEADER is to _________________ as PROFESSOR is to KNOWLEDGE.

7. ANGRY is to SCOLD as ROUGH is to _________________.

8. DENY is to _________________ as ACCEPT is to REFUSE.

> Read to find out if Stargirl decides to conform.

Questions:

1. How did Stargirl express her concern for the needy?

2. Why was Leo surprised when he saw Stargirl's house and particularly her room?

3. Why did Leo prefer weekends to school days once he began dating Stargirl?

4. Why was Leo infuriated by Stargirl's banner?

5. Why did Leo abruptly call Stargirl "Susan"?

6. What caused Stargirl to change her appearance and behavior?

7. Why wasn't "Susan" as happy as "Stargirl" had been?

8. Why was Stargirl excited about being a finalist in the oratorical contest?

Chapters 21 – 27 (cont.)

Questions for Discussion:

1. Do you think Stargirl's anonymous gifts were appreciated by their recipients?
2. What do you suppose was the rationale behind Stargirl's "stalking" game?
3. What do you think might have caused Stargirl to have a "three-pebble" day?
4. To what degree do you, like Leo, need "the attention of others to confirm" your own existence?
5. If Leo had come to you for advice about Stargirl and their relationship, what would you have told him?
6. Do you believe Leo should have tried to change Stargirl?

Literary Devices:

I. *Simile*—What is being compared in the following simile?

> Unlike Stargirl, I was aware of the constant anger of our schoolmates, seething like snakes under a porch.

Why is this an apt comparison?

II. *Symbolism*—What do you think the solitary mockingbird singing in the desert symbolized?

Writing Activities:

1. Write about a time when you or someone you know tried to make friends or become more popular by behaving in an uncharacteristic manner. Describe the situation and tell whether this attempt met with success or failure.
2. Write a dialogue that might have taken place between Archie and Stargirl on the subject of popularity.

CHAPTERS 28 – 33; MORE THAN STARS

Vocabulary: Use the context to determine the meaning of the underlined word in each of the following sentences. Then compare your definition with a dictionary definition.

1. After a lengthy <u>preamble</u>, the speaker finally got to her main point.

   Your definition ____

   Dictionary definition ____

2. As the storm lost force, the rain and wind <u>subsided</u>, and the sky began to clear.

   Your definition ____

   Dictionary definition ____

3. This tropical island, with its <u>abundant</u> vegetation and warm climate, supports many species of animals.

   Your definition ____

   Dictionary definition ____

4. Since I lost my script before rehearsal, I had to <u>improvise</u> my lines.

   Your definition ____

   Dictionary definition ____

5. Cinderella's jealous stepsisters <u>disparaged</u> her appearance and declared that no one would ever dance with her at the ball.

   Your definition ____

   Dictionary definition ____

6. Although my father is <u>reserved</u> in his praise, I know that he is proud of me.

   Your definition ____

   Dictionary definition ____

7. For several minutes after the magician's <u>mesmerizing</u> performance, the audience remained in their seats, silent and spellbound.

   Your definition ____

   Dictionary definition ____

8. It is presumed that <u>primordial</u> human beings did not speak in words but used grunts and gestures to communicate.

   Your definition ____

   Dictionary definition ____

Chapters 28 – 33; More Than Stars (cont.)

> Read to find out about the legacy Stargirl leaves behind.

Questions:

1. Why was the audience at the final oratorical competition stunned by Stargirl's performance? How do you know they approved?

2. Why were Stargirl and Leo shocked and upset when they returned to the parking lot at Mica High?

3. What caused the final separation between Leo and Stargirl?

4. Why did the students at Mica High become more vocal in their criticism of Stargirl?

5. What was the magical event that took place at the Ocotillo Ball? How did this event prove that Stargirl had made the right decision in choosing to be true to herself?

6. Why did Hillari Kimble and Wayne Parr suffer at the Ocotillo Ball?

7. How did knowing Stargirl change Leo?

8. Why was Leo optimistic about seeing Stargirl again?

Questions for Discussion:

1. Why do you think most of the students at the Ocotillo Ball became sympathetic to Stargirl? Why couldn't Hillari Kimble join the crowd?

2. Do you think the shunning would have resumed if Stargirl reappeared at school?

3. What do you think Leo meant when he said, "Nothing has changed. Everything has changed"?

4. What do you think was Stargirl's enduring legacy to MAHS?

5. Do you think the second gift of a porcupine necktie signaled Stargirl's wish to see Leo again?

6. Do you agree with Archie's appraisal that Stargirl was "a little more primitive than the rest of us, a little closer to our beginnings"?

Chapters 28 – 33; More Than Stars (cont.)

Literary Devices:

I. *Simile*—What is being compared in the following passage?

> As she got out of the car, the silver plate slid from her lap and rang like a dying bell against the asphalt.

Why is this an apt comparison?

II. *Symbolism*—What do you think Archie's burial of the paleocene rodent's head symbolized?

Writing Activities:

1. Imagine that you are Leo Borlock at age thirty and write a letter to Stargirl telling her about all you learned from her and how you have changed since high school.

2. Imagine you are Archie. Realizing that you may never see Leo again, offer him the advice you were never willing to give before.

CLOZE ACTIVITY

The following passage has been taken from Chapter Twenty of the novel. Read it through completely and then go back and fill in each blank with a word that makes sense. Then you may compare your language with that of the author.

She was bendable light: she shone around every corner of my day.

She taught me to revel. She ______________[1] me to wonder. She taught me ______________[2] laugh. My sense of humor had ______________[3] measured up to everyone else's; but ______________,[4] introverted me, I showed it sparingly: ______________[5] was a smiler. In her presence ______________[6] threw back my head and laughed ______________[7] loud for the first time in ______________[8] life.

She saw things. I had ______________[9] known there was so much to ______________.[10]

She was forever tugging my arm ______________[11] saying, "Look!"

I would look around, ______________[12] nothing. "Where?"

She would point. "There."

______________[13] the beginning I still could not ______________.[14] She might be pointing to a ______________,[15] or a person, or the sky. ______________[16] such things were so common to ______________[17] eyes, so undistinguished, that they would ______________[18] as "nothing." I walked in a ______________[19] world of nothings.

So she would ______________[20] and point out that the front ______________[21] of the house we were passing ______________[22] blue. And that the last time we had passed it, it had been ______________.[23] And that as near as she ______________[24] tell, someone who lived in that ______________[25] painted the front door a different ______________[26] several times a year.

Or she ______________[27] whisper to me that the old ______________[28] sitting alone on the bench at the Tudor Village shopping center was holding ______________[29] hearing aid in his hand, and ______________[30] was smiling, and he wore a ______________[31] and tie as if he were ______________[32] somewhere special, and pinned onto his ______________[33] was a tiny American flag.

Or she would kneel down and pull me down with her and show me the ants, two of them, lugging the lopped leg of a beetle twenty times their size across the sidewalk, as might two men, were they strong as ants, carry a full-grown tree from one end of town to the other.

POST-READING ACTIVITIES AND DISCUSSION QUESTIONS

1. Do you think Stargirl's true character is ever understood by those around her? Who in the novel seemed closest to such an understanding?

2. The theme in a literary work is its controlling idea. In *Stargirl*, the author explores several important themes, such as loyalty between friends, being true to one's individuality, the dangers of popularity, and the evolution of humanity. Choose one of these themes and discuss how it is worked out in the novel.

3. In the author interview in this book, Jerry Spinelli says, "Thank goodness for the outrageous among us." In what way is this novel a celebration of the outrageous?

4. Choose a fellow student or neighbor whom you do not know very well. Interview this person and attempt to find out what is important in his or her life. Write a brief biography of your subject. Then share it with this person and try to elicit whether or not you have succeeded in capturing his or her individuality.

5. **Cooperative Learning Activity:** The "point of view" in a work of literature is the author's choice of who shall tell the story. With a small group of classmates, analyze how Leo's viewpoint shapes our understanding of the events and other characters in the story. Discuss how the use of a different narrator might change the novel.

6. Although the author portrays the narrator as making the wrong choice, he is plainly tolerant of and sympathetic to this teenager. How does Spinelli manage to portray Leo as misguided yet likeable?

7. At the beginning and end of this novel, Leo is presented with a special gift. How does his response to each of these gifts, given over a period of fifteen years, suggest how he has changed and grown?

8. Has this book changed your need for peer approval? Do you think it is better to follow the crowd or pursue your own individuality? Is it necessary to suffer if you choose to go your own way?

9. **Literature Circle:** Have a literature circle discussion in which you tell your personal reactions to *Stargirl*. Here are some questions and sentence starters to help your circle begin a discussion.
   - How are you like Stargirl? How are you different?
   - How are you like Leo? How are you different?
   - Do you find the characters in the novel realistic? Why or why not?
   - Which character did you like the most? The least?
   - Who else would you like to read this novel? Why?
   - What questions would you like to ask the author about this novel?
   - It was not fair when . . .
   - I would have liked to see . . .
   - I wonder . . .
   - Leo learned that . . .

SUGGESTIONS FOR FURTHER READING

Blume, Judy. *Are You There, God? It's Me, Margaret.* Random House.

Cather, Willa. *Lucy Gayheart.* Random House.

* Cormier, Robert. *The Chocolate War.* Random House.

* Danziger, Paula. *The Cat Ate My Gymsuit.* Random House.

Eager, Edward. *Magic or Not?* Harcourt.

* Hinton, S.E. *The Outsiders.* Random House.

* Holt, Kimberly Willis. *When Zachary Beaver Came to Town.* Random House.

Kerr, M.E. *Dinky Hocker Shoots Smack!* HarperCollins.

* Konigsburg, E.L. *The View from Saturday.* Simon & Schuster.

Lasky, Kathryn. *Pageant.* Random House.

* L'Engle, Madeleine. *A Wrinkle in Time.* Random House.

Marie, Deana. *A Summer for Boys.* Vantage Press.

McCullers, Carson. *Member of the Wedding.* Random House.

Naylor, Phyllis Reynolds. *Alice Alone.* Random House.

* Paterson, Katherine. *Bridge to Terabithia.* HarperCollins.

* Peck, Richard. *A Long Way from Chicago.* Penguin.

* Salinger, J.D. *Catcher in the Rye.* Warner.

Some Other Books by Jerry Spinelli

The Bathwater Gang. Little, Brown.

Crash. Little, Brown.

Fourth Grade Rats. Scholastic.

Knots in My Yo-Yo String: The Autobiography of a Kid. Little, Brown.

* *Loser.* HarperCollins.

* *Maniac Magee.* Little, Brown.

Space Station Seventh Grade. Little, Brown.

There's a Girl in My Hammerlock. Simon & Schuster.

Who Put That Hair in My Toothbrush? Little, Brown.

* *Wringer.* HarperCollins.

*NOVEL-TIES Study Guides are available for these titles.

ANSWER KEY

Porcupine Necktie; Chapters 1 – 5

Vocabulary: 1. f 2. e 3. a 4. c 5. h 6. g 7. b 8. d; 1. elusive 2. weird 3. perpetual 4. sleazy 5. noteworthy 6. vague 7. ultimate 8. dramatic

Questions: 1. The gift of the porcupine tie prepared the way for other events in this part of the novel by hinting at mysterious doings and the friendship of an unknown person. 2. Among her conformist peers at Mica Area High, Stargirl immediately became the target of gossip because she dressed and behaved in an eccentric manner, had an unusual first name, played the ukelele and sang in the school cafeteria, and appeared completely comfortable with herself although she was in the midst of unfriendly strangers. 3. Leo and Kevin were especially excited by the presence of this new student because she would make an interesting subject for their in-school TV show, "Hot Seat." 4. Hillari Kimble hypothesized that Stargirl was a plant, hired by the school administration to stir up and energize the blasé student body. 5. The moonlight suggested to Leo "a sense of the otherness of things" by representing the imaginative and extraordinary in life; night was the time when Leo thought most of Stargirl because he could not fully conceive of her in the light of day, when practical considerations are emphasized and people are concerned with everyday matters. 6. Wayne Parr was typical of the Mica student body because he was blasé and refused to join in any school activities. 7. Spectators came to a Mica football game in the hope of seeing Stargirl perform as cheerleader at halftime as she had at a former, poorly attended game.

Chapters 6 – 10

Vocabulary: 1. e 2. g 3. f 4. a 5. h 6. c 7. b 8. d; 1. dormant 2. proximity 3. liberation 4. elated 5. amorphous 6. deceased 7. blithely 8. bafflement

Questions: 1. Leo and Kevin paid a visit to Archie Hapwood, paleontologist and mentor, because they sought advice about Stargirl. 2. Stargirl's solution to the problem of Hillari's birthday revealed that she was determined to follow her own agenda and clever enough to find a way to do so without openly confronting Hillari. 3. Archie's relationship to Stargirl was one of teacher to pupil; the two had also become friends and understood each other's nature. 4. Hillari didn't actually drop the rat down the stairwell because she realized how unpopular that would make her now that Stargirl had many admirers. 5. It was clear that Stargirl, who had originally been a pariah, had now gained great popularity. People flocked to athletic games to see her cheerleading, students vied to sit at her lunch table, and everyone imitated her attributes, formerly deemed eccentric. 6. Stargirl changed an amorphous, blasé student body to a group of individuals who energetically expressed their own individuality. 7. Several of Stargirl's acts of generosity were considered inappropriate by some of the townspeople because few understood her feelings of compassion; her appearance at the funeral created tension when her sorrow was seen as insincere and incredible; tension also resulted when the anonymous gift of the bicycle, after a near-fatal bicycle accident, was seen to be callous and thoughtless.

Chapters 11 – 15

Vocabulary: 1. f 2. e 3. a 4. g 5. d 6. h 7. b 8. c

Questions: 1. The recent fanaticism about winning games showed that the MAHS students had misunderstood Stargirl's lessons: she had tried to teach people to celebrate all victories either great or small. She had not tried to encourage individual team spirit or school spirit. 2. Stargirl's reaction to the MAHS vs. Red Rock game was consistent with her responses to other situations since in all cases, she had empathy with losers and victims and could not enjoy any situation in which someone was feeling pain or sadness. 3. Leo had a bad feeling before Stargirl was interviewed for "Hot Seat" because her popularity had already begun to wane; in addition, Hillari, her enemy, was a juror on the show. 4. When Leo said that Stargirl was taking the "Hot Seat" literally, he meant that she pantomimed sitting on an actual hot seat. She behaved in this manner to show she did not take the whole situation seriously. 5. Kevin and Leo were sorry they put Stargirl on "Hot Seat" because members of the jury, including Hillari Kimble, used it as a moment to vent their individual and collective rage against Stargirl's nonconformist behavior. 6. The MAHS students turned on Stargirl during their losing game with Glendale because she continued to cheer wildly in the midst of her team's defeat. 7. Leo ran from the lunchroom because he did not want the other students to see him talking to Stargirl; his actions did not reveal his true feelings but stemmed from his embarrassment at being seen with a girl for whom others had contempt.

Chapters 16 – 20

Vocabulary: 1. c 2. a 3. g 4. f 5. b 6. d 7. e; 1. dilapidated 2. immobilize 3. raucous 4. acquainted 5. barren 6. detached 7. treason

Questions: 1. When Leo said of Stargirl, "I was more comfortable with her as history than as person," he meant that he did not really know her; rather, he had viewed her as a larger-than-life figure who did memorable things and created herself as a legend. 2. In the enchanted place, Stargirl wanted Leo to attempt to transcend his body and personality in order to feel at one with the universe. Although Leo believed he had succeeded in finding some inner peace, he failed to achieve a complete state of tranquility as Stargirl had done. 3. Leo was at first unaware that he and Stargirl were receiving the silent treatment because he was in love; when he realized what was happening, he became anxious and upset. 4. Archie wanted Leo to choose his meaningful relationship with Stargirl over his casual friendships with school-mates; he tried to help him make this important decision by emphasizing Stargirl's uniqueness and connection to life's essential mysteries. 5. Stargirl and Leo disagreed about the importance of getting credit for good deeds because Leo assumed people wanted to be thanked for doing something good, whereas Stargirl derived pleasure simply from doing the good deed. 6. Leo realized it must have been Stargirl who had given him the porcupine necktie after he observed her giving anonymous, significant gifts to others.

Chapters 21 – 27

Vocabulary: 1. conferred 2. tentatively 3. extravagance 4. facetiously 5. distinct 6. zeal 7. jostle 8. confirm

Questions: 1. Stargirl expressed her concern for needy individuals by giving them anonymous gifts, such as balloons and hand-made greeting cards to improve their spirits. 2. Leo was surprised that Stargirl's home and her room were so conventional. 3. Leo preferred weekends because he felt free to enjoy being with Stargirl. On school days he suffered from being shunned by his peers who were critical of Stargirl. 4. Leo was infuriated by Stargirl's banner because it openly declared their relationship; he had been trying to downplay the romance around school in order to maintain some degree of acceptance by his peers. 5. Leo abruptly called Stargirl "Susan" to make her see that he was not wholly on her side; using her given name aligned him more closely with the students who shunned her. 6. Stargirl changed her appearance and behavior because she was hurt and shocked when Leo tried to force her to conform. 7. In her new personna as Susan, Stargirl no longer enjoyed the freedom to be herself that she had experienced as Stargirl, and her peers still disliked her. 8. Stargirl was excited about being a finalist in the oratorical contest partly because she was confident she would win, but mainly because she anticipated wild approbation from her peers when she returned victorious.

Chapters 28 – 33

Vocabulary: 1. preamble—preliminary statement or introduction 2. subsided—grew calm or sank to a lower level 3. abundant—plentiful 4. improvise—produce without preparation 5. disparaged—belittled; made less of 6. reserved—restrained in speech and manner 7. mesmerizing—hypnotizing 8. primordial—first; original

Questions: 1. The audience at the final oratorical competition was stunned by Stargirl's performance because it was completely idiosyncratic: she was relaxed and informal, offering a rambling discourse that tied together in the end. It was clear that the audience approved when they gave her a standing ovation. 2. Stargirl and Leo were shocked and upset at the sight of the parking lot devoid of people, except for two teachers and Dori Dilson: they realized that the students deliberately wanted to deny Stargirl's triumph to punish her for not fitting into their world. 3. Leo and Stargirl's final separation was caused by Leo's disappointment at Stargirl's decision to be her old self. 4. The students at Mica High became even more vocal in their criticism of Stargirl than they had been before because they now believed it was all right since they were expressing Leo's feelings. 5. The magical thing that took place at the Ocotillo Ball was the spontaneous and joyful merging of a hundred students who followed Stargirl's lead out into the fields and danced together in the moonlight. This event proved that Stargirl had made the right choice in accepting herself so that others could appreciate her unique gifts when she stopped trying to make herself ordinary. 6. Hillari Kimble and Wayne Parr suffered at the Ocotillo Ball because they and a few students stayed behind, unable to dance or socialize as most of the others followed Stargirl into the moonlight doing the Bunnyhop. 7. Knowing Stargirl changed Leo by giving him more spontaneity, a deeper appreciation of the small gifts of life, and an increased sense of wonder. He also attributed his career as a set designer to Stargirl who had shown him the enchanted place. 8. Leo was optimistic about seeing Stargirl again after he received a gift of the second porcupine necktie.